I dedicate this book to my dearly beloved Deva, partner in life, song, prayer and laughter. And as ever, to my Guruji, Master Osho who awakened within me the great gift of music and poetry and later brought me Deva.

I also dedicate the book to my son, Sam, and his mother, Diane, for the love and forgiveness they have so generously showered on me over the years.

And finally, to the beloved Gayatri Mantra — Homage to the Light within us all.

– miten –

Image on dedication page and page 34 by Giovanni Baroni
Image on page 1 by Andrei Kuzmenco
Images on pages 9, 35, 36 and 44 by Rishi
Image on pages 10 and 16 by DJ Pierce
Image on page 34 by Giovanni Baroni
Images on pages 26, 27 and 43 by Melinda Andreas
Image on page 8 by Shirley Cavanaugh
Image on page 40 by iStock
All others Deva Premal and Miten
Sanskrit text font by Wolfgang Fries

Published by Buster Bodhi Press, LLC

All rights reserved. © 2024 Prabhu Music Ltd

ISBN 9798327418202
Library of Congress Control Number: 2024942053

Design by Mark Andrew James Terry, Cover Photo by Rishi
Available on Amazon.com, Barnes & Noble online, and most online book sellers

in the garden of the mystic

songs of love,
wonder & devotion

– miten –

contents:

6   Dear Friends
8   Introduction

songs of love:

11   Till I Was Loved By You
12   Still Awake
13   Exactly As It Is
14   Bring Me Your Love
15   Home At Last

songs of wonder:

19   All Is Welcome Here
20   Garden Of The Mystic
21   Rain of Blessings
22   I Need A Beach
23   Second Chance
24   River Man
25   Who Am I Now
28   Native Son
29   Drop The Baggage
30   Four Angels
31   Humaniversal
32   Mother Inside
33   If I Die Tonight

songs of devotion:

37   White Cloud White Swan
38   Awakening
39   Rhythm of the Heart
40   Silent Space With You
41   The Greatest Challenge
42   Empty Heart
43   Deeper

Foreword

I was born into a happy family. I had no reason to rebel or to fight against the system.
That came later.

My early days were filled with wonder.

As I got older the wonder began to diminish — to dissolve — into a blurry haze of questions and problems that I couldn't even articulate, let alone consider or contemplate.

Something was just gnawing away at me, and I had no answer for it.

On the surface, if you didn't look too closely, my life was pretty good. I'd created a 'living' for myself in London's rock music industry — I'd made records, appeared on big tours, played to a lot of people . . . rubbed shoulders with some of my musical heroes . . . was married to a loving wife and I was father to a young son . . . I had friends to guide me when I was down, to challenge me, to comfort me . . . and yet . . . and yet. . . .

I think there comes a time in everyone's life when, for a moment in time, one stands at the crossroads.

I remember that biblical parable of the fishermen who laid down their nets and followed Jesus.

Sometimes, you just don't think twice. Those fishermen didn't appear to think about their responsibilities . . . I often wondered how the wives of those fishermen felt, how their kids felt when their father and partner just disappeared — up and left. Well, now I knew.

Just like those fishermen I walked out on the whole shebang.

Didn't even look back.

Imagine how much guilt, shame and darkness you carry around with that load on your shoulders.

I had some serious inner work to do on myself in order to survive the shame and hurt I'd caused.

I'm going to cut a long story short right here. My son, who was three years old when I left him, is now one of my best and dearest friends. He asked me to be his best man at his wedding — and he even named his son after me.

My ex-wife, Diane, his mother who was left alone with a broken heart never rebuked me, never shamed me . . . I can only imagine what she went through. And thank god, over the years we have all pulled through.

She forgave me. It was a miracle. And now she never misses a concert when Deva and I play in England. We always share quality time with our son and our grandchildren whenever I visit England, and she even plays a hot ukulele in a ukulele band!

But all the forgiveness in the world doesn't add up to much without self-reflection.

And this is where Osho comes in. His meditation techniques, his loving community, his compassionate grace, his insightful teachings were all on offer . . . all I had to do was to hold out my hand.

As he always said: It's up to you. Nobody can do it for you. I do not have followers.

I took that leap into my darkest self, fought tooth and nail with my demons during the meditations that Osho suggested, and emerged a new man, living his second chance, with a new name and a clean and empty heart to reference a song in this book.

In a way I'm living a happy ending, because through the grace of the master and my own struggles, I feel that I'm ready to let go of this earthly body whenever my time comes.

It is my 77th year as I write this and to quote another song from this collection: If I die tonight, that'll be alright, I did what I came here to do.

There are no regrets.

I was taken by the sweet perfume of the flower of life; the blessed Gayatri Mantra which I heard for the first time, through Deva's voice, in Osho's sangha.

In the garden of the mystic.
And that's my story in a nutshell.

I hope you, dear reader, fellow traveler, kindred spirit, will find some semblance of solace, not only in the words and the rhymes, but also within the spaces between each word.

With Love,

—miten—

Introduction

As a practicing poet with four books of published poetry and a long career of involvement with poets and poetry as a teacher and mentor, I am often called upon to judge poetry contests. Over the years I have developed an ear for what makes a poem great, and what qualities were in the poems that deserved to be contest winners. I read thousands of poems, listening for the magic of words that opened my heart, made the world a finer place, and deserved to be heard by the world. Listening to Miten's music over the years, I realized that his songs had all of the attributes that were evident in the finest prize-winning poems.

His lyrical genius, craftsmanship, delightful and perfect use of rhyme, rhythm and meter thrilled me. His images had power and were beautiful. His hard-earned spiritual wisdom spoke to me directly and reassured me that we are all loved and watched over by a higher power. I wanted to see them in print so that I could have access to them and to him whenever I wanted to take the time to enjoy his poetry. I realized that it was a desire on my part to let everyone see the world through his eyes. The book you are holding in your hand is the result of our collaborative effort.

Welcome to the Garden of the Mystic.
Enjoy your stay and come again, often.

Joe Cavanaugh, President
National Federation of State Poetry Societies

songs of love

"It is like throwing a stone in the silent lake – the first ripples will arise around the stone and then they will go on spreading to the further shores. The first ripple of love has to be around yourself. One has to love one's body, one has to love one's soul, one has to love one's totality."

— Osho, The Invitation, Discourse #30

प्रेम के गीत

TILL I WAS LOVED BY YOU

I never was loved so deeply
Never was loved so true
Never was loved so completely
Till I was loved by you

I never knew I was blessed but now I do
Never knew what I was missing
Till I was loved by you

Angels all around me
I had angels at my door
There were angels in the kitchen
Meditating on the floor

Guides to guide me
And friends when I was down
But still there was something missing
Till you came round

I never was loved so deeply
Never was loved so true
Never was loved so completely
Till I was loved by you

I never knew I was blessed but now I do
Never knew what I was missing
Till I was loved by you

Time is a fiction
I am not afraid
Time can only take away
The things our minds have made
But love's glory is no small thing
And I knew it - when I heard you sing

I never was touched so deeply
Never was touched right through
I never loved so completely till I loved you
I never knew I was blessed
But now I do
Never got to see the man in me
Till I was loved by you

STILL AWAKE

I open up my eyes
She opens up her senses
Dropping our defences
We're letting go

I open up my arms
She opens up her voice
We make a conscious choice
To be here now

So even when we fall asleep
We are still awake
And even when we close our eyes
We still see the light

I open up my life
I feel the spirit move me
Funny how I used to be afraid
But now I'm hanging with the clouds
And I'm sliding down rainbows
Anywhere the wind blows
I'll be there

So even when I fall asleep
I am still awake
And even when I close my eyes
I still see the light

This where we come from
This is where we go
This much I know

So we open up our hearts
We were not born to follow
Life is just another hollow bamboo flute
So let the music call our ancestors
   and teachers
They know where to reach us
They know who we are

So even when we fall asleep
We are still awake
And even when we close our eyes
We still see the light.

EXACTLY AS IT IS

Oh the flame in my heart
It burns for you, my love
Like a river, burning red
At the close of day

And the wheel of my life
It turns with yours, side by side
I have no choice
I simply love you that way

It's like that
And it's like this
It's exactly as it is
It's a natural affair
There's no mystery there
It's exactly as it is

And the healing light
From the blessed sun
It shines for you
Beloved one
Shining on this river
Burning red
At the close of day

I've seen that river so still
I've seen it roaring in flood
You are the river, running in my blood
And I rejoice
That I have loved you this way

It's like that and it's like this
It's exactly as it is
It's a natural affair
There's no mystery there
It's exactly as it is

I simply love you

BRING ME YOUR LOVE

Bring me your love
Bring it on home
Bring me your body
Your blood and your bones

Bring me the water
From your wishing well
Bring me your longing
And your temple bell
Bring me your love

Bring me the rhythm
The rhythm of life
Bring me your darkness
Bring me your light
Bring me your love

A small blade of grass casts a shadow somewhere
Even butterfly wings have the power to move air
Everybody's naked beneath the passions we wear
So bring me your love

Bring me your poem
The one you recite
The one that you whispered
In that still sacred night
Bring me your love

HOME AT LAST

You will always be my darling
You will always be my bride
You will always have the best of me
On this you can rely
You will always be my sweetheart
No matter what comes to pass
Because home is where the heart is
And tonight I'm home at last

Home at last
Home at last
Home is where the heart is
And tonight I'm home at last

You will always be my baby
You will always be my girl
You will always be a part of me
You're the heartbeat in my world
You will always be my lady
No matter where we roam
Because home is where the heart is
And tonight my heart is home

Home at last
Home at last
Home is where the heart is
And tonight I'm home at last

Yes you will always be my sweetheart
You will always be my bride
You will always have the best of me
Cross my heart and hope to die
You will always be my lady
You're my future you're my past
Home is where the heart is
And tonight we're home at last

Home at last
Home at last
Home is where the heart is
And tonight we're home at last

songs of wonder

"The experience of wonder is such that everything stops. The whole world stops; time stops, mind stops, the ego stops. For a moment you are again a child, wondering about the butterflies and the flowers and the trees and the pebbles on the shore, and the seashells – wondering about each and everything, you are a child again."

— Osho, The Dhammapada, The Way of the Buddha

आश्चर्य के गीत

ALL IS WELCOME HERE

Broken hearts and broken wings
Bring it all, bring everything
Bring the song you fear to sing
All is welcome here

And even if you broke your vow
A thousand times
Come anyhow
Step into the power of now
All is welcome here

See the father and the son
Reunited here they come
Dancing to the sacred drum
They know they're welcome here

See the shaman and the mighty priest
See the beauty and the beast
They're singing "I have been released
And I am welcome here"

I stood alone at the Gateless Gate
Too drunk on love to hesitate
To the winds I cast my fate
And the remnants of my fear

I took a deep breath and I leapt
And I awoke as if I'd never slept

Tears of gratitude I wept
I was welcome here

So bring your laughter
Bring your tears
Your busy lives
And your careers
Bring the pain you carried for years
All is welcome here

Freedom is not so far away
There's just one price we all have to pay
Live our dreams until they fade away
And let them go.

Live our dreams until they fade away
And let them go

GARDEN OF THE MYSTIC

I saw a rose
In the garden of the mystic
I didn't pick it I thought of you

I saw a bird
In the garden of the mystic
I watched it as it flew...
And I thought of you

I thought of a love without any name
I thought of a fire without any flame
I thought of forgiveness without any blame
Without any shame

And only love remained
In the garden of the mystic

And I heard music
In the garden of the mystic
I heard laughing and crying
Living and dying too

And I joined the dancers
In the garden of the mystic
Round and round and round and round
And round and round we flew
Dancing in the dark
Dancing up a spark

Dancing in the heart of the hurricane
Till only love remained
In the garden of the mystic

I watched the sun rise
Above the garden of the mystic
I watched it as it grew
Like the love I saw inside of you
I saw you there
Sunlight shining in your hair
I got down on my knees and I said a prayer
In the garden of the mystic

RAIN OF BLESSINGS

Rain of blessings
Pouring down
Kiss the earth
And this holy ground

Holy water
Heaven sent
Rain of blessings
Our sacrament.

Rain of blessings
Sing your wild song
Mighty god of thunder
Beat your heavenly drum

Beat the drum of mercy
Beat the drum of forgiveness
Beat the drum of freedom
I'm bearing witness

Rain of blessings
Holy water
Bless the mother
Protect the daughter

Bless all creatures
Great and small
Rain of blessings
God help us all

I NEED A BEACH

I need a beach
I need a place in the sun
Somewhere out of reach
Somewhere I can run free
Free from a world full of trouble and pain
Free from a world going insane
I need a beach

I need a place in the shade
Somewhere I can sit down
And forgive myself
For the mistakes that I made
Free from a world full of trouble and stress
My spirit's strong but my mind's in a mess
I need a beach

It doesn't have to be in Saint-Tropez
I don't mind
Venice Beach down in West LA
That'll do me fine

Copacabana, Malibu...
Any old beach'll do

I just need some sand
Under my feet
Give me a little rockin' band
Playing the reggae beat

Call me crazy say I'm out of touch
But it's the human touch I'm missing so much
I need a beach

Take me down to Blackpool town
Southend-on-Sea
Arillas Beach clothing optional
That's fine with me
I've got some good friends down in Byron Bay
They've got some beaches down there
That'll blow your troubles away

I just need some time
To get myself straight
Slow down my mind
And meditate

Meditate on a world full of fears
Meditate on this ocean of tears
I need a beach

Wash my spirit clean
Dancing with my sweetheart
In the moonlight waves
That kind of scene
Oh Lord, if you can hear me please
Send me down an ocean breeze
I need a beach

SECOND CHANCE

I hung my hat on a wishing tree
I asked for one wish — I could've had three
But I only asked for what I needed

I could've asked for money, riches and wealth
But all I really wanted was to find my self
Unaccustomed as I was to seeking

And my heart whispered inside
And the moon rose and the angels sighed

And they said, "Here comes your second chance
You'd better believe it
Open up and receive it
Here comes your second chance
Take a deep breath
This is your second chance"

Make peace with your mother, your father too
Make peace with the stranger inside of you
And forgive yourself for things you tried
And failed to do
Embrace your anger
Your lust and your greed
That's how we drop the things that we don't need
Pick up a musical instrument
Go out and plant a seed

That was my heart whispering inside
Welcome she said
You're home and dry

And here comes your second chance
You'd better believe it
Open up and receive it
Here comes your second chance
Take a deep breath
This is your second chance

Well the years went by and my wish came true
And I find myself here with you
I had to climb a mountain
There was no way around it
We all come and go like waves in the sea
Each with our own responsibility
To leave this world more beautiful
Than we found it

And that's your heart whispering inside
You can trust your heart
You know, it never lied

Here comes your second chance
You'd better believe it
Open up and receive it
Here comes your second chance
Take a deep breath
This is your second chance

RIVER MAN

Close to the water that's where I am
The river is my teacher
Close to the water that's my plan
The river is my teacher

Clean or dirty
That's just the way she goes
It's not just about the water
It's all about the flow

I am the river man

Close to the water I'm on holy ground
The river is my teacher
I love to hear her singing I love that sound
The river is my teacher

She always takes the path of least resistance, I know
It's not about the distance
It's all about the flow

I am the river man

I could've been a carpenter
Carving Buddhas out of trees
I could've been a fisherman
But I couldn't steal from the seas
So I became a river man
And in one's and two's and three's
I carry you over to the other side

Close to the water
That's where I'll end my days
The river is my teacher
Where words of wisdom come
In most melodious ways
The river is my teacher
And she'll be rolling long after we're gone
It's all about the rhythm of life
It's all about the song

Song of the river man

WHO AM I NOW

Who am I now
After that kiss
Where is the ground beneath my feet?
Who is this fool who cannot sleep?
Thinking of wild flowers and rain showers
And a love so impossibly sweet
Who am I now

Who is this man
Who walks through the world
Who put that smile upon his face?
Who filled him up with amazing grace?
He's dreaming of wild flowers and rain showers
Far removed from the human race
Who am I now

Who is this man
After that kiss
Nothing appears to be the same
Once he was cool now he's aflame
Dancing through wild flowers in rain showers
He can't even remember his name
Who am I now

NATIVE SON (For my son, Sam)

Go lightly on this fragile earth
We are all strangers on this shore
Remember what your life is worth
And what it was we came here for

And hidden deep within our heart
There's a light that shines on everything
On the right and the wrong
On the weak and the strong
On the prayers and the songs that we sing

Go lightly on this precious land
We're part of everything we see
We're the teardrop on the ocean
We're the wind that whispers in the tree
The wind that cries in holy rage
At the deeds and the damage we have done
For how little we care for the life that is there
Go lightly my native son

Go lightly on this sacred earth
Go lightly on your way
You are among the ones who took
A second birth
And we are blessed more than words
Can ever say

Maybe sometimes your heart is broken
But it's nothing that love cannot repair
And with the gifts that you bring
Remember one thing
It's the love for yourself that you share

DROP THE BAGGAGE

We've got to drop the baggage
We've got to travel light
We've got a long road ahead
And we'll be moving day and night

We've got to drop the baggage
We've got to let it go
We've got a long road ahead

Some friends of mine living on this earth
They've got a hunger for the inner search
They've got the eyes of the mystic
And they're walking on the path of love
It's the way of the heart and it don't come free
Living and dying consciously
They got the eyes of the mystic
And they're walking on the path of love

We've got to drop the baggage
We've got to travel light
We've got a long road ahead
And we'll be moving day and night

We've got to drop the baggage
We've got let it go
We've got a long road ahead

Like an arrow!
Like a warrior's spear!
The days of the conscious revolution are here
We got the eyes of the mystic
And we're walking on the path of love
No promises - no guarantee
But it can happen to you if it happened to me
I've got the eyes of the mystic
And I'm walking on the path of love

FOUR ANGELS

Four angels watching over me
Four beloved strangers I can feel but I cannot see
One on my left — one on my right
One up ahead — one leading me into the light
And I'm not afraid no more
I'm not afraid no more

Four angels so I can't go wrong
I just do and let thy will be done
I get up in the morning lay my head down at night
And I tell myself, man, you must've done something right
'Cos I'm not afraid no more...

Not afraid to be afraid
Not afraid of who I am-Not afraid to stand up
And be a man in love

Four angels even in my sleep
Day and night no matter what company I keep
Some people say that fools rush in where angels fear to tread
But I'm the fool who woke up with an angel in his bed
And I'm not afraid no more...

Not afraid to live
Not afraid to die
Not afraid to laugh
Not afraid to cry...

God bless these four angels

HUMANIVERSAL

Ever been lonely?
Ever felt out of place?
Ever cried yourself to sleep at night
Praying for descending grace

Ever danced alone in the moonlight?
Dancing like there's nobody there?
The whole world could be looking on
But what do you care?
You're dancing your prayer

Humaniversal
We're all reaching for the stars in the sky
Humaniversal
You and I

Ever been to India?
Seen the world from ground zero
13-year-old mother with a baby in her arms
Knocking on your taxi window
Lights change and you leave her standing
In the road
Still her eyes come back to haunt you
Wherever you go

Humaniversal
We can all hear her baby cry
Humaniversal
You and I

And after all it's only life
We come and go in the wink of an eye
We say hello we say goodbye
Is that all...?

And what about the Dalai Lama...
What about that smile
Simple monk from the roof of the world
Living in exile
He can't go back and he can't go home
What does that say to you and me?
He speaks with love and compassion
Even towards his enemy

Humaniversal
Say a prayer for his people
When you're driving home tonight
Humaniversal
Say a prayer for him
When you turn out the light tonight

MOTHER INSIDE

I said a prayer for the homeless
I pray no life is lived in vain
I lit a candle — blew it out
Stepped out into the pouring rain
I went looking for the mother inside

World turning
I cried tears of redemption and forgiveness
Crossed that river
Looking for the witness
Reaching out
Reaching for the mother inside
And the rain fell down like the tears of the virgin
Tears of joy for all souls emerging
As we reach for the mother inside

Sun rose at midnight
Everything changed
My plans and my schemes
All rearranged
As I went singing for the mother inside

YEMAYA
SHAKTI MA
DURGA MA
MARIA MA
JAI MA! JAI MA! JAI MA!

We're all the same under the skin
Unprotected, searching
Searching for the mother inside
Birth and death in every breath
One lover after another
As we search for the mother inside

Mother Earth
What did we do
We took too much of you
We were reaching out for the mother inside

IF I DIE TONIGHT

If I die tonight
That'll be alright
I did what I came here to do

And if I'm gone by dawn
No need for you to mourn
I did what I came here to do

Over the mountains
Over the sea
Me and my sweetheart wild and free
High on the wings of the Gayatri
Forever blessed
Forever blessed

So when I'm deceased
You can say well at least
He did what he came here to do
So when they close the door
On all that went before
Be sure you did what you came here to do

songs of devotion

"Devotion is not a path. Devotion is the death of the personality. That which is mortal in you, you drop of your own accord; only the immortal remains, the eternal remains, the deathless remains. And naturally the deathless cannot be separate from existence – which is deathless, which is always ongoing, knows no beginning, no end. Devotion is the highest form of love."

— Osho, The Rebel, Discourse #20

भक्त के गीत

WHITE CLOUD WHITE SWAN

This is no ordinary love affair
I love somebody and there's no one there
White cloud and an empty chair
It always was and it always will be

White cloud, white swan, white light
From beyond the beyond
White cloud, white swan, white light
From beyond the beyond the beyond

I lay my life into your healing hands
Offer up my love making no demands
Trust in something I don't understand
I'm letting go and I'm sailing free

With a white cloud, and white swan
And a white light from beyond the beyond
White cloud, white swan, white light
From beyond the beyond the beyond

How do you thank the ocean?
How do you thank the wind?
How do I thank you Osho?

This is no ordinary love affair
I love somebody and there's no one there
White cloud and an empty chair
It always was and it always will be

songs of love, wonder & devotion

AWAKENING

We are awakening
To the calling of the Mystic
Awakening
In the flowering of the heart
Everybody here
Melting into presence
Overflowing effervescence
Rising in love

OM SHANTI SATCHIDANANDA

OM SHANTI OM

We are awakening
To a long forgotten memory
Dawn is breaking
Waves are coming in
Everybody here standing in wonder
Beneath the rain and the thunder
Rising in love

OM SHANTI SATCHIDANANDA

OM SHANTI OM

We are awakening
To this perfect imperfection
Awakening in the wonder of it all
Everybody here
Part of each other
Sister and brother

RHYTHM OF THE HEART

I can still remember the first time our eyes met
I could feel the approach of a hurricane
It's a time I will never forget
And in one timeless frozen moment
That remains to this day
You looked into me and I could see
There was nothing in my way.

It was the rhythm of the heart
It was a fire shining through
And I'm dancing to that rhythm
No matter what I do
It's the rhythm of the heart
And there's only me and you
Dancing to the rhythm of the heart.

Now in one sense that time is over
Your body is long gone
But the love we shared is still alive
And that's what leads me on

I don't need to believe in love
I can feel and I see it's right here
You gave me back my innocence
And the will to disappear

Into the rhythm of the heart
Into the fire shining through
And I'm dancing to that rhythm
No matter what we do

It's the rhythm of the heart
And there's only me and you
Dancing to the rhythm of the heart

SILENT SPACE WITH YOU

I woke up laughing
Strange but true
I was dreaming of a white swan
In that silent space with you

I saw a colour reflected
Silver and blue
I saw that white swan in a flash of light
In that silent space with you

It's more than romance
More than sexual
This is a one-to-one
Full-on connection

I don't need to hear your voice
To feel your heartbeat
I don't need a body
To contain this love

Across the shining water
That white swan flew
On and on and on and on
In that silent space with you
And as the longing increases
The light comes shining through
And I see my only release is
This silent space with you

THE GREATEST CHALLENGE

I can see you
When I look beneath the surface of my life
Here in the silence
Where no sound has ever been heard
Calling me on
Like a song in the distance
Calling me on
Like a fire in the heart
And to answer your call
Is the greatest challenge of all

I can see you
When I look around the circle of my friends
I see you in their eyes
The same way they see you in mine
Calling us on
You're the song in the distance
Calling us on
You're the fire in the heart
And to answer your call
Is the greatest challenge of all

I keep asking myself
What is this jewel in my hands?
I keep seeing my mind
Slip through my fingers like sand
If not now, when?
If not here, where?
If not me — who could I be?
Calling me on
Like a song in the distance
Calling me on
Like a fire in the heart
And to answer your call
Is the greatest blessing of all

EMPTY HEART

So many roads I wandered
Only to find they all led to my door
So I don't have to search no more

I take the water to the thirsty
I sing my songs to the empty sky
I pray the rains have heard me cry

I've got this empty heart that I can't explain
No longing for love no sweet pain
No voice I hear in the still of the night
Just an empty heart full of light
Resting in emptiness

I tried to name the nameless
I tried hard to understand
But when I closed my fist well, of course I missed
There was nothing in my hand

I used to think I knew where I was going
I used to think we had to get somewhere
Now it's enough to watch the river flowing

With this empty heart that I can't explain
No longing for love no sweet pain
No voice I hear in the still of the night
Just an empty heart full of light
Resting in emptiness

Deeper
Into the heart of love
Letting go into the mystery
Rising in Love

songs of love, wonder & devotion | 43

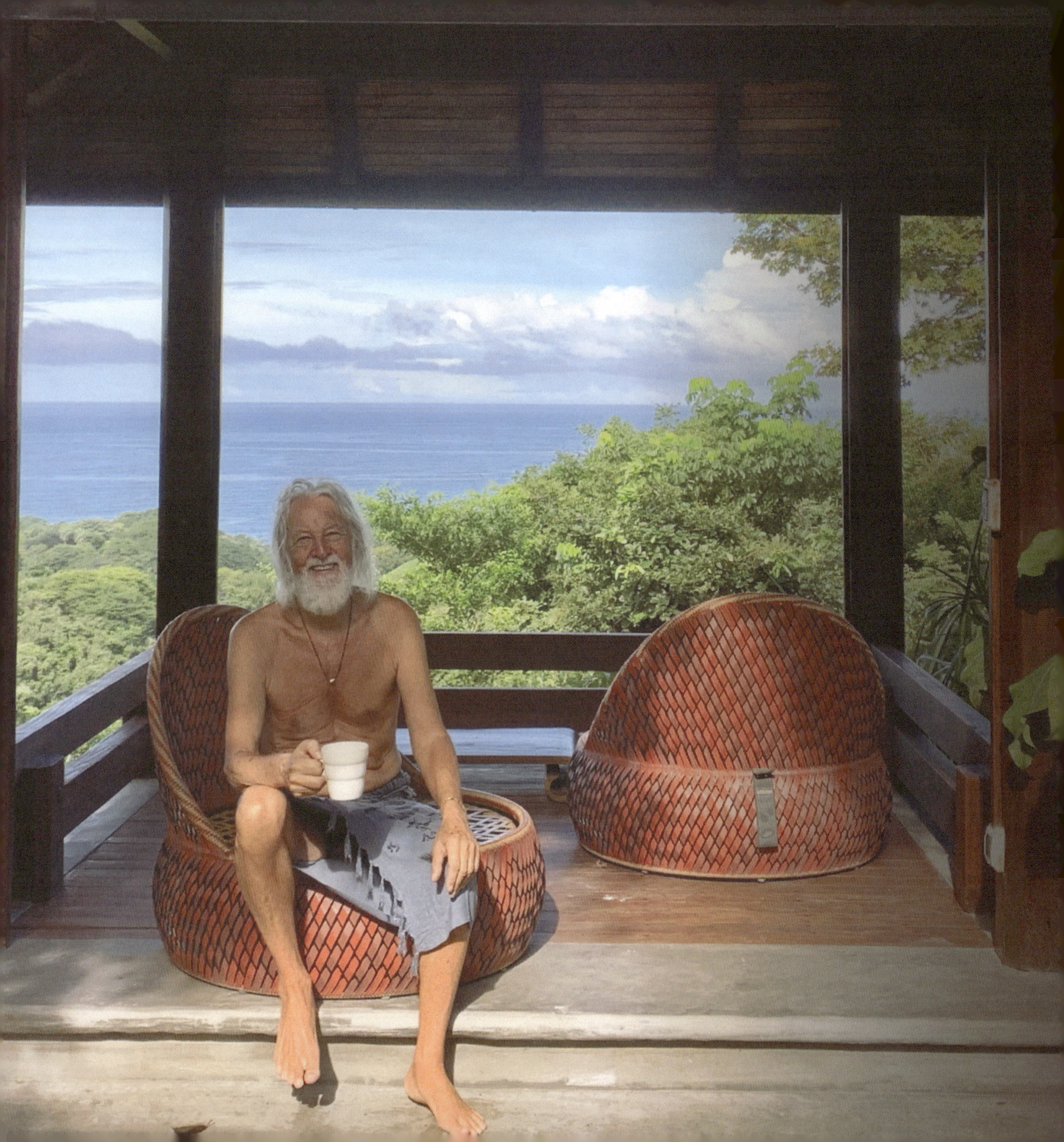

Thank you

Special thanks to my friend and brother, Joe Cavanaugh for his inspiration and guidance. His love for my songs created a book I never expected to write. Thanks Joe.

Love and thanks to Mark Terry for the design of this book.

Also many thanks to my beloved Osho Community and our Gayatri Sangha for nurturing these songs through the past forty years.

To continue the experience, listen to the Spotify playlist:
Miten — The Garden of the Mystic

Printed in Great Britain
by Amazon